View from a Borrowed Field

Meghan Sterling

LILY POETRY REVIEW BOOKS

Published by Lily Poetry Review Books
223 Winter Street
Whitman, MA 02382

https://lilypoetryreview.blog/

ISBN: 978-1-957755-19-9

Cover art: Detail from "Gay Head," Albert Pinkam Ryder

Table of Contents

View from a

Borrowed Field

Stone Fields with First Snow

Out of my past flew a crow,
its wing broken, its wing night-blue as ink
that had written my dreams, that had woven the stones
that rolled their code in the body's black mud.

When the crow slept on the ground, it came to love
the rock that was its bed, its stone dark head,
the sky hung upside down over the field,
the rivers that bent their way toward a hollow moon.

I first saw the fields in a dun-brown cloud, the early winter
like a sleep that had come over me, my eyes certain
that all was ocean, roughed by storm. I saw the stones
had heaped themselves like gods across the land. A crow

with a broken wing standing at the road, watching us
as we walked the fields, as we poked the frost with our boots.
We could live here, I thought. This broken earth.
This land of hard hard rock. We could plant and make things soft

or come to ruin--right here. The crow hopped on
its singular path down the road past the barrens.
Where the back is broken, love can grow. Where the land
is broken, the cold comes and makes of it a coat.

Something of the Sky

Ghost Story

It's winter, and I'm dreaming of Vietnam again, basket boats of fish and flowers,
old lovers, my grandmother's face, the way time shoots forward and backward,

how I'm riding the Junks across Halong Bay's sepal green skin, my body
like a stranger at the market, handling Rambutan with its messy fringe,

my body a ghost in a season of heat. Where did she go, that stranger?
Here, it's a borrowed spring, cold then colder; it won't make up its mind

if buds are to blossom or retract, if we can ease into our bodies or swim
in our clothes. I remember a spring when I had love, when I didn't know

what was coming. That time is also now. Already, the losses have begun to tally
in the sky's notebook, a sun in the center like a splotch of ink. I don't mean God,

I mean how the earth makes its own sense—ships that once sailed off
the horizon's edge were still sailing, even when we couldn't see them,

even if for us, the ships were gone. Maybe my old loves are the ships.
Maybe the stranger on the junk, her solitary life strung like a thousand moons,

also sails, just in a different direction, her smooth hull carving water
in twin lines, casting salt that brines every ocean that can be crossed.

Before School There Are Icicles

Clattering on the frost, a dozen of them that gave

and fell together, music like tin chords on strings of wind,

their piano notes ringing across the tunnel between buildings,

and we are delighted. Echo of winter morning, sharper

for all the lonely air, no birds to fill the sky, no clouds,

only the vibrant blue like our heads thrown back, branches

in ice completely as though struck by a spell, and we sing:

the sky is a million mirrors, the sky wears the tips of the branches

like the diamond frills of the Elizabethans, and we crown it queen.

Shadow of sun across the glass driveway, and I try to nudge my

daughter toward the car, playing freeze tag, desperate not to slip.

She asks for icicles to suck, so we leap from tree to tree as I break off

the dangling bits, cold threatening to cut exposed skin, flesh of my hands

raw, each tender icicle like a finger prick of good for her to taste—

something of the tree in it, something of the sky.

Big Ones

I'm dreaming of money and it's awkward
because I want the feel of silk on sandblasted skin,
my flesh torrid, unblemished by work.
My horse sense tells me
I'm worth at least twice what I'm paid,
if only my bosses would agree.
My bosses are: memory, the dead, schoolteachers,
the bully on the playground each year
a different blonde boy.
Money could buy me something
to fill the spaces that feel nothing—
an icy puddle, a sky heavy with storms
where my hands sought the sun.
Money could buy me the Golden Fleece
to shield my loves from my February heart,
black snow in piles along a highway.
I want money to buy a heart. Or someone
to clean my house so I can write.
Yes, how it feels to touch it, greasy paper
like the scales of fish, fat as a cat in a pile,
in a wallet, although the money I really want
is invisible, the smell of a clean house,
the smell of coming snow.

Everything that Grief Can Make You Hold

I wept into the cat bowl crusted & spent, its dried meat folded
with dander & dust I hadn't gotten to sweeping,

groceries bagged, stacked three deep
on the floor, a ticket for an expired inspection

from a stark-bald cop, my daughter hungry for play
when my joy felt tapped, my face haggard in the moments I took

to brush my teeth, which in our house we call 'self-care'.
Up the night before, I watched a bruiser of a sky

play tricks with the streetlights, purple halos like black eyes,
branch-tips laden with winter seed-pods cast against the screen of the ceiling

& thought about my father until daylight, my daughter's breathing
soft as a bird's breast while the room bloomed into a morning that spun

too fast, my little daughter saying *that's just awesome*
with her hands on her hips like she gets it all, everything, our cars

driving until the cops shine their blue lights into our tired eyes,
my father's decline accelerated into tenderness,

his body breaking into tufts of fraying milkweed
we catch in our teeth between fevered breaths.

After Reading Keats' "Ode on Melancholy"
in Late February

No, no, don't throw yourself under the hood of the tanning booth
or spend your nickels on fashions just to alleviate ennui.
You will still slip on ice when you walk to your car, your black coat
crusted in salt from brushing against its once-blue exterior.
You can attempt refuge by driving South, maybe reach
New Hampshire. The roads will cough up soot, the dust weaving itself
inside the white ribbons of the snow banks, silver walls of the guardrails
moving like the ocean just beyond sight. You must remind yourself
it's only five weeks until April, a month whose name always delights,
despite what Mr. Eliot said, a month that promises change.
Hard little buds like teeth appearing on the tips of branches, the blossoms
on the cherry trees a pink smack in the mouth. And though you are still
under the weight of February, avoid the wine, gin, vodka, tequila,
chocolate, pasta, loaves and fishes that call your name
as you pace the apartment like a rat in the night. This is a month
for asking questions when things get hard. Where do you go
when all around you is frozen sharp like the inside of an oyster shell?
How many ways can you describe gray? How about ice? Who are you
when the light has gone? When your neighbors' roofs are buckling
beneath heavy snow? You must find out. Put down the ice cream.
Fall on your face in the ice. Taste deep of the ashes left in the can.
The only way out is through.

Trawl

All the men I pass are mine.

      The streets teeming with them, their fur, their wit's end.

How everyone is a piece of a man

      I've known before. How they still move

through me, bits caught in my net--

      a screen, a sieve. I make a mosaic of them,

the detritus left arranged on a mat to catch the light

      with the sky so high and blue today it is singing.

Today, men are wind chimes, men are cars wheeling

      through the snow while cold air rushes off snowfall

in an effort to hold everything back from falling.

      Today, men are toy towers, are lampposts.

The man across the street shrugs his mornings

      loosely, shovels himself out. The ice a mirror cast

like a tie slung around his neck. The man my father,

      wearing his mornings like a navy suit.

The man my mother, wearing her anger

      like a bold red lip. Even in clothes, the men are naked.

Even in women. You can see them in their houses at night—

      circling each other like tigers, sitting at their tables,

lying on their couches, crouching below the windowsills.

      You can see the way winter moves between them,

the way they claw the walls.

Mother Mirror

She was house poor, mortgaged to the moon, light-starved,
married to a closed door, furious. No outlets, nowhere

to tell the story. It outed in hailstorms of rage, as it will.
I forgive her for this. Twenty years later, I am house poor,

steeped in rent, light-starved, married to a window, seeking solitude
more than I can find, more than is allotted to someone

with a small child. I see now: children take some of you
every day, along with their milk and bread, pieces inhaled

as they scream into the silence, as they scatter their crumbs in your bed.
There are things you think you know, the way I knew I would be giving up space

to bring my daughter into my life, the way I really know that now,
driven mad by love for her and also craving quiet with my entire body,

like everything I've ever desired fully: lovers, coffee after waking,
to be beautiful, and now, a vacuum around me, morning deep in gray dawn

and nothing but the soft hiss of the heater, rain on the roof
and the hush of my typewritten words like a lullaby.

What is Enough

The poem ends with an image. The moon, the birds. Has the poem earned
the right to these images, I ask on a bright and cold Sunday afternoon,

after dreams of old friends woke me early? Has the poem earned the words
to describe love? The moon is horses, its feet are birds. There is a field of fruit trees

where the birds have replaced the apples in the tallest branches, singing like diamonds
beneath the earth. Has the poem discovered anything, apart from you, still in love

with everyone you have ever loved, still in love with old dreams? The house is an ocean,
the moon is a songless bird. I wake up each morning and feel a fool. I miss people I
knew

before, and they appear on the page. My dreams show me beauty I can almost
taste, my hair heavy, my arms impossibly long, like the necks of cranes when I straggle
awake,

born from sleep that showed me the faces of lovers I was too afraid to love. My poems
translate dreams into pictures that live outside my body, the moon is a missing tooth,

the birds on the shore peck at glass they think scraps. My poems say my body
is a winter shadow, power lines across a horizon cold and straight as a knife,

birds crowded on a pole above the street, where the moon is snow,
friends are birds, dreams are long cold lines of light, always reaching.

Throat

The stripped snow turned white
under the breath of the junco's wing, the song
of the cold calling under a canopy, long
branches dim with December light.
I was small then. The frost didn't touch me.
It shoves me now, chilling deep to the skin under my skin,
the place where my heart and bones wring out their kin
from the glacial ice that has broken it, utterly.
The blossom clings to the branch. The trees cling
to the field, its roof of lonely stones. If only snow
were this small, this soft in the throat, this low,
could we recognize the sorrow in the junco's wing?
My daughter, wise at 4, says the world works just so:
We are safe, mama. We are safe. You can let go. You can sing.

A Walk After Being Let Go

There was a maple thick with cardinals like apples
at the park yesterday, their wings filling the space,
their voices singing in a discordant racket, like children
shrieking as they run. I was staggering under the future,

a ghost draped in wet wool, slushing through ice-melt
to see the holes in the pond worn by the warming weather
like moths. In a month I will be jobless. In a month,
there will be hard little buds like raised fists along the branches.

In a month, the days will open wide as the mouths of tulips,
as a cat's rising yawn. Sunlight will rise like a tongue
licking the sooty streets clean of all the winter grime,
and I will finally be free to do the work I've always wanted—

releasing the red birds trapped in the page.

Despite How Much We Say We Hate Winter

Like mother's milk, the snow has scent
our bodies seek. We hunger for the black sky

bright against the white
revealing the shape of things, our edges,

ghosts, the meanness of ice, and winter's too-slow return to light
late at night. The sky threatens this sinking earth

as we walk along the coast,
my family and their dreams lost in the waves,

the shtetl they fled, and all in their graves.

I don't know how to explain to their memory
what I have done with my time here, how I have tried

to love this place, to save this place,
fed too as I've been by love and struggle

by loss, and all of this beautiful snow
the joy and cruelty of snow, the way that winter contains us
in its endless fields, its massive hands,

the way it brings us closer to our beginnings—
dark, light, and altar.

Things Barely Known

After a Diagnosis of Postpartum Mood Disorder

There are three of me: keeper of ghosts, keeper of songs,
keeper of flesh. I am busy changing, a new leaf that has turned
from yellow to green overnight. My daughter sleeps, her skin
of cinnamon, her hair the under-feathers of the starling.
Every morning is a turtle's shell—domed with nerves, shot
cloud-white like lightning when my hand brushes rain
on the windowsill. Follow me down the stairs to the place
of weeping before anyone else rises. It is in woods so thin
you can touch the roofs of houses strung with last night's rain
like bells. Hear them clang, where the street meets the trees.
Hear them grow, the rain getting heavier inside each drop,
pulling with its water-weight, mothers preparing to birth.
My thumb leaves no imprint in moss. My shoes settle lightly
into mud like the feet of birds. When I kneel at the trunk,
my praying is silent, creeping along the tree's veins like sap.
I know I can be better than I was. I can forgive my mouth
that was bound, my hands for too easily slipping.
I can forgive my eyes for not knowing how to mourn my dead.
I can place a fallen bird's nest in a crook of the oak that's slow
to unwind from winter, fight the sleep that wants to pull me
into its mouth. I can imagine the field I will plant with cherry trees.
I can hold my daughter to my tree bark skin and sing.

Shrine

In spring, the wind almost kills
with its fists. I dream I die and shine
in fields the color of puddles after a freeze,
tree limbs waving in the reflection
above my daughter as she shows me
her paperchain, the letter A strung
in endless joining. I want to hold her
longer than she wants to be held.
She bucks, then pats my face, her fingers
gentle as new grass. She points to the trees:
there, the chirps of sparrows to the south.
Or maybe they're wrens. Bronze birds
the color of naked bark, their twittering
like her quick lips on my cheek. How I
would give her everything as long as it's quick.
I am impatient for purple crocuses to show
their faces, for buds to crown the branches
like a million babies being born. Last night
I lay awake, tallying: Fourteen years before
her room empties, becomes first a shrine,
then an office with a bed or a pull-out sofa,
the air sighing around the furniture. I run and run
but I can't catch up— she blows past me all gold
and rose and banana skin, that sweetness I want
to keep hold of if only I could remember
forever the feel of her small hand.

Bronze

We have come this far. Circle to 8.
Circle to the year of the ship. Circle to Arches,
to house buying, to giving birth.

Circle to the Great North. To the weight of work.
To our child running naked in socks down the hall.
To the house we dream: porch, water view, claw foot tub, space.

Circle to our lives utterly joined, like the fittings
of a boat that wear and wear, without corrosion.
Your body a boat propeller, whirling, circling the saltwater.

Your body, Roman statue, long and smooth,
cast to the bottom of the ocean. Your weight, moonlit,
a copper color, as if your own body blushed at its nakedness.

The air cool on skin like tin. The air coming in at the sides
of the blankets, rushing in to touch you. Your voice like a cannon-barrel,
rending stone, remaining even when the seas rise to meet it.

And we are in need of nothing. Not the missing water view
or the absent fields of wildflowers. Not the back yard thin as a thread.
Not the crescent moon or the snow banks crested with soot or the frozen lake

we stagger over. I wouldn't tell you that you're anything less
than everything that is more than enough. Than the bird. Than
the nest. I have looked and looked, and all I can find

are the thinnest cracks on the surface of things, like the world
is a thick sheet of ice that cannot break, as though everything
we touch is pliable, porous, remaining whole.

Poem After Bitter Dreams

There are places inside of each other we can't touch, don't want to,

all the years spent pretending you weren't comparing me to your first,

the one with the face and the rage, all the years pretending I wasn't

damaged goods. What I didn't know was how much we store up to serve

to the next contestant. Every time I see a waterfall, I know I don't measure up.

Every time I dream we buy a house, it is infested, has hollow floors,

moldy carpets. Last night, I dreamt we were thieves: breaking and entering

our former house and a shop at the mall, stealing a seven dollar purse.

Our daughter was part of the getaway, twisting with rage in her car seat

as we circled a parking lot, nowhere to go, no money for gas. She was one again,

angry she couldn't walk, howling with fury at sky, leaves, roads,

the smooth palms we held out to steady her—too proud to accept,

too desperate to refuse. Last night, I dreamt that my ex was eating at a dinner party

in our former house, and you and I watched like ghosts on welfare, the orange carpeting

bowing in spots, brass chandeliers and spotty mirrors jutting out from every surface,

like detritus in a pawn shop. There is a world where I can afford to live,

but I haven't found it yet. There is a world where I am steeped in a tea of rose water,

a world where I am loved the way a child loves a butterfly that has landed on her wrist,

delicate, delicate, tenderness of rain on leaves, of things barely known.

Artists in Quarantine

Whether we ever touch again like we did
those years we stormed and burned, years
that led us to the commitment we made
and made again when we gave birth.
How I relied so utterly on you to steer the ship,
to get us through the darkness of so much new,
and now with each day blank, this pause that gives us
stolen time will end, and work will call us back to other faces,
other lives. How will we look back on this time?
I will admit that I've been taking greedily of my own heart,
in strangled bites, a half-starved thief whose greatest hunger
is for time. When the world resumes and you head back
to danger and absence, remember that I kissed your neck
the times I passed.

Aninut*

It will be a boy, the psychic assured.
See there, he hovers around you now
waiting for his invitation
into your life

and after many weeks of holding back blood
I knew he had come
Abram or Amir or Aarav,
little Ani

the way he sat with me that night hushed and lit
by the fire   small as the worm moon

and we listened together for that gentle pulse of ocean
to rise in my veins, for him to announce his life
inside mine
a faucet drip the only rhythm held
but for the wood rustling as it softened to ash

and later when there was a dream of a spark
like metal on metal
that brought with it the familiar red
it was the signal of my body's refusal to keep him, or his
to remain

*Hebrew for sorrow

The Year Our Daughter Was Born

So much had to change. The body I had known, with its illness,
its scars; our marriage rhythms, all dependent on my keeping
the beds weeded and edges clean, powering through days with the energy
of a thousand flower girls, all those trodden blossoms.

We had been walking the hidden garden that spring she took root,
the skin of our feet soft with the mosses' names: Haircap, Heath Star,
Tamarisk, Goose Neck, Glittering Wood. The light had arced its back
and landed in our laps as we sat on the bank watching the river tangle

with thrown stones, coming to rest again in its fish-eye shape,
framed by a daylight moon. How it would part and rumble around the rocks,
then come back to tender rushing, its glass threads running toward the needle
of the falls. How my body had been busy, quietly healing all that year

with its stitches and sutures, so done with harboring wounds,
so ready for something beautiful to come of its wounds.

Self-Portrait with Sparrow Song

Green fields leaning towards gray water

and the song in the underbrush just beyond

the tree line. You were bidden here. Song of the cedar branch,

song of the summer morning. Fan your feathers out

like your grandmother's Hermes scarf, a silk tail

of pink and brown squares. Follow it up the soft back

nearly broken by love. Song of the curtains closed to the sun.

Follow it to the place where the bus would drop you

along the road with its peepers, its trophy wives

and masturbators. Song of the squeaky bed. Follow it

across the atlas in a zig zag until you come to the man

in the ficus, his sex in his hands. Song of the runaway,

the memory housed in our shared bones. Follow it to the house

that would birth you. Song of your daughter, waking.

Taking your face in her hands like the moon at its fullest.

Follow it until you come back to this branch, heavy with summer,

light with needles about to drop. Song of the sparrow, the wren,

their voices blue as the ash of all your years set to burn.

Full Circle

A poem came to me once, but it skirted the sheet covering
my grandmother's legs. How I clasped her feet to warm them
between my hands, but they didn't yield like they did on Saturdays

when I used to rub her feet with lavender lotion while she beamed
in gratitude. Now it's twelve years since her death, since she pushed
the air away as if to make room for her flight, not that she believed

in such things as *flight* or *souls* or *heaven*, but the way she looked at me
as I rubbed her legs I see again in my daughter's face when I've spent
all night with her, holding her hand for hours although my arm falls asleep

and aches as if shot. She is so grateful in the morning, she holds my face
in her hands with a tenderness sharp as cracks on the surface of an egg.
This morning, I almost couldn't bear it, loving her that much,

being that loved, having her look into my blurry face and see
sunshine, snowfall, invisible threads lifting us up into skies
red as fire, which is to say, everything she thinks is magic,

and how I ached knowing that change is coming for both of us
fast as a bullet. And then I remembered the poem I didn't write
on my grandmother's deathbed and I saw that it had returned,

that it is always returning, in the way my grandmother's hands
pushed at the air as though conducting music, in the way my hands tried
to warm her feet, in the way my daughter now holds my face in her delicate hands
and I then hold her face in my clumsy ones. How my daughter's face is everything
I never thought I would have again, the love I felt long ago staying bright enough

to light another, and another, and another.

Enough to Sustain

View from a Borrowed Field

Once I came near enough to the earth
to taste its skin—the smooth of stone

to the tongue, like waiting for nearness,
for someone to come and pick me

as if my eyes were apple blossoms.
I imagined that I would find a field

to fall into: Columbines with crooked stems,
Foxtails leaning sideways in wind,

sunlight gleaming from a broken spoke,
and name that field my own: Azurite, Onyx,

as if my space was all mineral, all tooth
and earth. There would be something solitary,

something infinite, a deposit of belonging
staked into soil. I would dress up for it,

wearing my difference
as a stone wears its edges, as seed

wears its skin, ready to be carved,
to split open.

Married Life, the Smell of Toast, Toothpaste

Your unwashed hair, peonies so deeply blooming
they hang open like the hinges of a barn door blown open,
earl gray tea with that tang of bile, fresh tar in the street.
Our street is a series of broken panes the wind blew loose,
our street is lined with spent lilacs and their portent
of the human face. This wind speaks of love but we aren't listening—
there's a true-crime podcast, its tin voice thin above
the slosh of the dishwasher. How clean are the counters
beneath hands that just held a bluebell bouquet, how fresh
is the wind that blows the neighbor's pride flag into a whirr of color.
The world looks just as it must—a cat scratches at the door,
the oak leaves whirl in circles by a wind that blows them,
how the wind blows every which way like the years that press us
with their air. How we erode like beach sand, how we quicken
like a pulse. We made love today like we did seven years ago,
just married. How tired we were, in awe of ourselves.
How tired we are now, while the street sheds us with bits of gravel
and fresh pavement along the grass lawns, while the street wears us
like a smudge of color on its lips. How the world was ours for awhile,
while we weren't watching. How the world was ours when we wanted it less.

The First Days

The empty hammock on the porch across the street
spins like a pinwheel as if holding the body
of a sleeping child, or a feather in wind that drew the snow
across the city late into the night,
the bare spring earth now deep in cover,
something to blanket and fill these empty days:
windows looking out to white, blank as we shutter,
succor families with meals, baths, crafts,
anything to keep a loose grasp on our old lives.
The house has never been so clean, the floors
stripped to bone with disinfectant, poisons
locked tight under sinks, hidden away from small hands
that could be harmed. The bleaches stink to our marrow,
the alcohol dredged from the back of cabinets tightens
across palms that shrink from touch, each forgotten motion
a wince, and we hide from each other, as if in our homes
we can find the only solace in strange times,
in the faces of those we love, in the wanting that never ends.

My OCD is Now "Good Hygiene"

A sudden desire to clean the mirrors. Anything glass,
as though the me that I glimpse as I pace, busy myself
in the silence could survive this better for a purer silver shine.

How I try to keep this house clean, to keep this bug
from landing and making itself at home. Everyday
watching my daughter, waiting to see if symptoms will come

(was that doorknob sprayed? has she washed her hands?)
and what if I didn't act quickly enough, to wipe down faucets,
handles, shit, if I forget a sliver of shadowy corner, my whole family

depends upon this diligence. My anxious childhood rising
before my eyes. This whole sickness like a judgment:
what kind of mother would I be to allow this thing into my home?

What kind of woman? I want to fight it off with my gloved hands,
curse it behind my mask, slap it raw, toss it to the curb with the bad men
and old fears that have dogged me into my adulthood. The house

is haunted with the possibility of germs. My knees bruise.
My hands bleed. I dream I kneel before a statue of St. Francis,
but while he preaches I fixate on his soiled stone feet.

Lockdown Day 1,000,000

Meanwhile, we are running low on milk. It is all my daughter
wants to drink, even in her bath, she wants it to run sticky
down her chin and chest, clouding the bathwater gray,
like her belly is the Niagara Falls of Milk. Sometimes
she pours it deliberately into the tub, just to watch the cloud
swirl and settle, even when I tell her milk has become precious,
don't waste it. She doesn't understand—to her, it is not wasted.
Meanwhile, my husband isn't playing piano today, he is reinstalling
the shower doors and caulking, his hands eager for work after weeks
of meandering over the keys. Meanwhile, the men in yellow continue
digging up our street, day after day. I should follow their lead
for how to mine for poems now, the way we seek them out
inside ourselves with so much effort, or sometimes no effort at all,
when there is a death or a bad dream, or folding socks triggers a thought
that's less mundane. Meanwhile, the mine seems tapped. Like today.
Day after day in lockdown. Day after day looking out at the workers
bronzed faces, their yellow vests, cigarettes dangling out of their mouths,
but even they seem to find something new to dig each day, the gravel to move,
the pipe to hoist, the dozer to scour the dust, the way my daughter
shouts for her milk, drinks deep of that same sour flavor when it arrives
and finds new joy in it, enough to sustain, every time.

Brooklyn the Color of a Hospital Gown

Tonight the sky is moonless black as my tongue
after curry and Pepto Bismal tablets when I ran
to the hospital on Dekalb convinced I was dying
all summer, reading Calvino into the cold gusts
of the air conditioner that jutted over twisted roses
quivering with the drip drip drip of ice blue condensation
as if this machine had tears enough for all of us
while I would sing into the fan unit, watching the vortex
shed from the trailing edge of the blades slice my song
into pieces. Where was the sense? A certainty of dying
like the odor of elephants after a rain and how I had become
only ashes of who I had planned to be, now a hypochondriac
at the ER when I found a lump on my leg, or a blackened tongue,
or the rain that cooled everything for just a moment,
the air becoming clear as a church. I knew I would be leaving soon,
since we couldn't admit to each other there was no moon,
only hazy stars above the stalls of the carriage houses
on Waverly when I would venture out to move my car,
the streetlight a finger in my eye, the moon a bridge waiting
behind clouds thick and pink as bismuth, the boom boxes
on the stoops playing all the old songs, only smaller.

Self-Portrait with Winslow Homer and a Raincoat

Four months in, and all is mottled as fever, sharpness of wind in teeth,
needle that tattooed my arm. Not enough fresh fruit or greens.
Everything steeped in salt, crusted in the stuff so it won't rot.

Out here, we are bigger—rainwater, brine, detritus bobbing along surfaces:
wood and water, sand and water, swept here and there like buckets of slop.
All day and night we swap off to stand watch, to mark time, measuring

the memory of a day on land, memory the only thing from land that keeps.
Life back home was a lull, quiet as stone. You can hear the house ache.
I remember being shut in rooms that stayed still, stillness like a ghost

that followed me into dreams. How we chase noise out of our homes,
how we drive out the wet. Here, the damp is a friend you're forced to make,
the horizon a toy we pull the sky along with, before us, behind us, the line of a life.

But I miss my family's voices. When we near land, the gulls crying out
are my children, the surf roaring against the boat's hull is my wife's breath.
Those moments tear at me, unlivable. So many months yet to go.

What else to do but become rough as sandpaper: mussel, cockle, quahog.
Live each day silent as a pearl being made in the oyster's belly,
watch the sky and breathe into the salt, committed to ride this one through.

Vaccine Tango with the Red Red Rose

In the dream, Covid like a maraschino cherry in my arm,
traveling down veins full of syrup, red as iron, red as
a bead in my ear. You shook with rage in the driver's seat,
almost collided with a woman asking for change. No one
was wearing a mask anywhere, not in the library at my
book signing, not at the vaccine clinic, not on the street
bustling with basket weavers. The Bandaid on my arm
was holding in my sickness like stage fright. Swallow
and step, little pox. Covid was making me bold,
the way it bounced around inside my body
like a game of Arkanoid, bounce off the paddle, rebound
to the other cell wall. Red spikes like a Rambutan, o
that soft white center like sinking one's teeth into an eyeball.
You weren't laughing, hated my book, my squirming cells,
the virus a stone in my throat, a cherry lozenge swallowed
and caught on the uvula, swinging like a punching bag in those old
Loony Tunes. Covid tap dancing around under my skin
like a bug under a rug, as you railed and wept, ending our marriage.
While again, Covid peeked out from behind my red-rimmed eyes
and snickered, and again, Covid rolled its round hairy body as if
my body was a ball pit, lunging from edge to edge with the glee
of a kid at Chucky Cheese.

How NSSI is a Hammer, a Door, a Knucklebone

When the day begins with the familiar madness—fists to flesh of self-harm
hidden inside the wrist of shame, this urge to beat, to knock and pummel my brain

against a wall, usually pushed by something small: my daughter's refusals, my husband's
withdrawn and walled face. This morning, after a long night, my daughter spitting her

medicine onto my chest sent me out of the room, slamming my milk drawn hands
against my head, ramming my fingers into my skin, out of ear-shot, silent but for that

satisfying thunder against my skull like the pull of gristle from bone—how it quiets the noise,
soothing like a ragged purr. My mother pulled chunks of things—plaster from the wall, her hair.

I too am a container that is over-full. I am a container for their wants and it is spilling
into the thirsty dirt. My family wants my attention as though I can make flowers bloom

at a glance, the medicine staining my hands pink as a lie, the medicine spattered in fuchsia dots
across the ceiling, out of reach of my sponge. I remember the hands, how they seemed to come

like tigers from behind a tree, but the rage like white spit on freckled lips—I know that now.
It lives with me, a sleeping cat that wakes to feed, wild with hunger, teeth displayed.

And still. I feel broken, a container barely holding everything: the tears of my family,
bills like a flood, the search for a piece of land to plant with sun-starved seeds,

my daughter's fury, these poems festering like scratches left by dirty claws
and all I can do is tear open a hole in my skin so that the whole vessel doesn't explode.

Afghanistan is Your Fault

And also my fault, the way I pretend the world
isn't happening, organizing my closet by color, by
season, touching the soft fabrics instead of reading the news.
The way I'm back at my window where I watch
the neighbor's pride flag's colors reflect the mood
of the moment, how it was twisted when the pandemic
started, how it has been twisted since the pandemic
continues, but right now it is flattened, faded
in a late summer light that aches with coming autumn,
its stripes of many colors pulled taut by the wind
like a dress set to dry on a line, while the people of Afghanistan
are rushing the airports, they are swarming the tarmac,
they are surrounding the airplanes as if they can leap onto a wing
and be lifted away from what's happening to their lives,
the way the women are facing a terror bigger than tears
or the death of the earth, looking into a hole where the sun
had just been blooming, wrapping themselves again in their black
that had gathered dust in the back of their closets, the way their black
is mourning for the textbooks that will be burned, the way their black
is mourning for being walled again in their homes, the way their black
is mourning for the sun as it dims and the earth grows cold and all the birds
give up their plumage to die beneath the folds of their colorless wings.

Sound and Smoke and Nothing

Sonnet for the First Blue

Today I want to spear the sky with my tongue, press it deep
behind my knees, beneath my neck, tuck it between sheets of paper

and crumble it into the folds of my skin where my elbows
meet the flesh of my arms. I want to hold it there until the blue quakes

with want and I release, roll it over tangled in clouds like sheets
and allow my skin to scent its sour musk. Let me harbor its slow breath,

this first true blue all year, and wear it like sparrow wings along my reaching
body, that blue the shepherd of light and all the fucks it gives,

the urge to climb, the power to exert wind over earth, to pummel grasses
with our long weasel backs, horizon line like the skin of bulbs pressed

against rock, stalks reaching to break through the edge of soil. This expanse
like the corner of canvas, ripe for making, steady in its stare.

Blue so tight you'd think it was tin-plate, thin as metal at the periphery,
sharp enough to draw blood.

Pyrocumulonimbus

Astronauts say space smells of walnuts;
acrid, sweet, with a hint of ozone, like wine
sipped in an empty room. Lately, the scent is toasted,

so much earth engulfed in flame. Seen from above,
it's almost beautiful, a symphony— small orange dots
swallowed by masses christened by the Greek: clouds born of fire.

They cross over and under in monstrous braids of smoke,
racing across the forests— Blue Jay, Feather, Slink—
tearing through a landscape that once sheltered me

from despair. I remember looking out over the Oakland redwoods,
deep into dim mountains gold as ink in a slanted sun, and felt
the world's beauty was enough to live for.

Now all is soft falling ash, ash we might mistake for snow
but for the enormous heat, the way ash sticks to the body
like memory, like grief.

I'm Not Thinking About the End of the World

Because I'm too worried about the hummingbirds and the 20 foot Basking Shark
they just found in Casco Bay. Yesterday's trees become tomorrow's factories,
tomorrow's factories become today's furnace, registering at an impossible
98 degrees. Once I slept in a field of dandelions and woke up with my mouth
stained yellow, watched by a Blue jay with a stem in its beak. How can the birds
find their twigs and tufts if everything is clapboard and cladding? Let me wallow
in the violets, loll in the leaf blades of the lupines. Let the groundswell spill its blooms
in a summer fever between the razed riverbanks. The fields are an empty room
echoing with Chopin's nocturnes. The fields are an echoing clock. I'm not thinking
about the trees because there is one honey bee clinging to the wood of the kitchen
windowsill. What small life will I rescue today? The moon is the same width as my thumb,
the same width as the hole in the screen where the bugs get in. This time last year,
it was a firefly, lost or resting, its one bright bulb flashing in the dark. What will we do,
as we feed the hummingbirds who search for last year's lupines, with their tiny hearts
that beat and beat, when there are no fields left?

Chickadee

My daughter sang softly this morning,

respecting the sleep of others like a little nun,

whispering her vespers to the dolls she cradled

on a pillow in the middle of the kitchen floor.

I savored her quiet, her voice like wings,

delicate as branch-tips just beginning to crown with buds.

Her song was the black throat of the chickadee,

hopping from limb to limb, crested by blue sky

like all the love that had been waiting

once I stopped searching and started looking.

But that's the way the sky is. Always there,

but still, a revelation on a spring morning

when all is quiet enough to hear it hum.

Suppose I had decided to stay childless?

I'd be listening to the birds on the lines,

desperate to find anything to make me feel

as tender as my daughter so easily does,

singing in hushed tones to her monkey and owl

wrapped in a blanket of old towels.

Ghost Guns

Meanwhile, Biden announced that he has resolved to deal with ghost guns,
ghost, because they cannot be traced. More like ghost-maker. I imagine

transparent gears, metal bits like smoke, the bullets wispy, translucent,
gossamer-light. A play thing, dissolving in the hand that wields it.

Components ordered from disparate dealers, A Frankenstein weapon. Meanwhile,
we can't even deal with legos tossed like casings across the living room floor—

we can never find all of them, and a red brick always ends up jabbing an innocent foot.
How can the government do any better? And now my daughter is nearing school-age,

Pre-K in the fall, and I want backpacks and pencil cases and that delicious eraser smell
for her, but behind my want looms the threat of shootings, caution tape across a playground,

a dresser full of clothes a child will never wear. As I fall asleep, I imagine her
at morning circle, singing songs in her tiny screech, then gunfire, and I'm not there

to throw my body across hers. I already feel I am to blame, along with these guns,
these ghosts, haunting my mother-mind. Meanwhile my daughter has to be in this world.

Grocery store, gas station, soccer field, school. I cannot control any of it,
even the guns have become spirits, receding into sound and smoke and nothing.

Loon Stabs Bald Eagle through the Heart
the Same Week George Floyd Is Murdered

Every mother knows this fear. Dreams that have kept me up nights:
a thick-necked stranger grabs at my infant daughter, the roar
of rising waters wresting her from my arms, and now, a policeman
kneeling on her neck as she calls my name. She is 3, and I still dream
she is a newborn, my DNA dictating me to organize every part of my life
to protect her, my body becoming a shield. It just happens: you look
into the face of your child, petal-soft and gaping like a fish, and you resolve
that you would kill for her. The loon was no different.
The chick she lay, that she carried across waters, cradled in her wings,
grasped to death by the eagle who thought this was just another answer to hunger.
But we mothers know the brutal acts possible—the fingers that stroke our infant's hair
would stab out a man's eyes without joy, urged to murder by the simple fact
of animal justice. And the grief that propelled the mother's beak to pierce
the eagle's heart as fast and clean as a bullet is the grief that all mothers
flinch to mention, and the man on the ground, as breath failed him,
calling out mama as he was murdered by a policeman, is the voice that haunts us—
every mother who heard that call cries out in answer: *Darling, we are coming.*

Animal Dreams

I am ready to be every animal—crocodile, koala, skink, lemur.
I dream my skin is scales, fur, feathers, a tender cover.
I dream I walk the streets of Rome with my hoofs sharp
against cobblestones, that I am curled beside the radiator,
my tail as pillow, my ears alive. I am ready to be every animal

that didn't survive my ownership—a rabbit that ate its way out
of a metal cage, a borrowed hamster, a dog that turned out to be
vicious, a wild cat we thought we could contain. I see the rows
of tombstones in the pet cemetery down the street: Bailey, Cleo,
Maple, Buddy, Max, and I dream I am living the simple life

of the petted—sleep, wake, eat from a bowl, business outside,
play. And again. And then, confronting my owner in punctuations
of love, the silent nearness. I dream I am a cat held in a lap
and the heat is love. I dream I am a goldfish and the magnified eyes
watching me over the glass bowl's lip are love.

I am ready to love everything like that,
the way a dog will nudge a ball with its nose over towards
its owner's feet, the way a cat will paw at one bright spot of sun
on the floor, circle it twice, and settle into light.

Moths

Dive down a Blue Heron's neck, vernal pond
and its gaping mouth, frog croak, threat of birdwing,
the Luna moths draping the screen door,
black flies swallowing air and light in their gathering.

The mockingbird song like a thousand lit matches. And now,
how like the frogs we have become, living life underwater
as we navigate work, as we learn what it is to be parents,
to give utterly, finishing each day ragged as a cast-off skin.

Time is moving faster. We hardly see each other, waves rushing up,
rushing out again, seasons shifting without pause—schedules and pickup,
dinners and bedtime, the waves driving us together and then apart.
Again, the pond swallows the reeds in its spring surge,

the birds have to dive deeper to get at the minnows, the moths bat
at the porch-light in wild attraction, though they knock their heads
on the lamp a thousand times and nothing comes but the singe of wing.
And yet, I admire their ferocity, their love of light stronger than even

their bodies. Tell me we are more like moths than the birds,
who leave their nests to rot in the April rains. Tell me
we can approximate the moths' stubborn will— moving again
and again towards each other until we're stunned blind.

A Door to Somewhere Else

Rear-View

And then you come to realize that you have chosen your life,
where instead of croissants in your 19th century Parisian walkup

it's Cheerios and sippy cups, soon to be backpacks
and soccer cleats, followed by lip balm and mall drop-offs.

You aren't questioning what's next anymore—examining maps
of the Pacific Northwest to see where a random move could take you,

scrolling ads for camper-vans or Airstreams, searching crowds
for the eyes of your life-companion—you have found him

and he sleeps hard, his face deep in a pillow as you write this.
You know now that all the waffling about having a baby

was just an attempt to create a fork in the road. Should I? *Should I?*
The question was your answer. And sure, you used to scamper

to Peru or Vietnam or Mexico or Europe easily, quickly,
packing your Lonely Planets and hiking boots,

those unfamiliar cities and landscapes bright as the wings of birds,
your solitude mirrored in the vistas you encountered, Lake Como

and Lucerne spilling all that blue at your feet, alone in the present tense,
your skin vivid with new light. Only now it's the little things

that send you careening, like the apartment empty for a few hours
this morning, almost too much in the vastness it offers—

sunlight hovering like a white moth, the memory of the turn
you didn't take.

O Medusa

Countless, the time I spend imagining my way out of a paper sack,

where the sack is solid rock, bills, stones, inherited rage,

the hoist and heft of the daily task of work, of being mother, of being wife.

Hand-holding, notes to self: spinach, toilet paper, laundry, garbage out Thursdays,

she likes her milk cold. Countless, the hours I write numbers and lines to

figure out how to make it all run—the house, the job, the meals,

moonlight in the pines, a heap of leaves to turn into a craft. What a

wizard, what a saint. But truly, I'm wound tight, my shoulders

pinned to the sky, my body steel, my face patched like a tire.

Even the moon gets tired of shining. Even the pines get to hide in the dark

sometimes. Even the cat. I found her under the bed yesterday, sitting on a guitar,

half of a stuffed mouse hanging from her maw. There wasn't any room,

or I'd have joined her. Somedays, I dream of Iceland. Others, of Greece,

or any place where I don't flinch to hear my name, where I don't hate the sounds

of being alive, because there are fewer. O Medusa, where is power

when I need it? Bring me your particular poison, help me funnel my dreams

into a basin of witch water, help me refocus my gaze so I can relish my husband's

smooth hands, my daughter's lips on my cheek. Be the rage so that I can be what I must.

My Grandmother's Pockets

Brimming with blood that bloomed over the curved earth, torch of the bombs,
a rage that my grandmother spoke without translation in the ancient tongue,

shaped by the wind that blows through holes in the city walls and pocks the earth
with stones like olive pits. This was the story she offered with one hand in her pocket—

sorrow that followed her here from the East with its dry sockets and apricots.
But I didn't want that story. Instead, I waited for light like a dog, my legs raised

to the gold of summer sun, shamelessly bare, my legs stretched out to be touched
by one long blade of grass that grew from an abundance of green. I looked away

from the news, the land with our people, racing from death, or stepping right in.
The fields ripe with shattered bones and the tongues clicking "tsk, tsk" at the girl

overseas averting her eyes. Here, it was summer, and I could pretend I forgot everything
but green, soft as the belly of a bird, or the airplanes that striped the air like a clock,

cracking the clouds clean every hour. Here, where a tulip was my long painted finger
as it reached its stalk deep into the vase. I have desired like that every day of my life,

with all of my cells sprung and solitary as if I lived in the center of the moon.
Today even, I use my desire like armor, breastplate and greaves. I have turned my back

from my grandmother handing me the ancient hates she kept in her skirt. I have done this
to avoid knowing what it is to place a tulip on my father's body cooling in its casket while

the bombs arc and roar like slow-moving meteors in a sky yellow as a cat's eyes,
their roars drowning my grandmother's vindicated cries from the cement wall of her grave.

Panacea

My daughter rises as if lit by fire, as if
there is no bridge between sleep and wake.

Immediately, she wants stories and I pull them
out of my bleary mouth. She wants songs.

She moves in, stares deep into my sheet-creased face
and wants to lick my nose. She is everything

I was before, and she is more because she is her
and is all that is silver with light—the surface

of a pond at night, full of moon, the first enamel sky
of spring high as a spire. I have lost myself in love

for her and it is good. I wanted to be better than I was,
and it took a girl, a mountain, Maine, this constant bright attention

and soft hands shoving me into gladness, that bossy
high-pitched voice ordering me into joy.

Sleep Deprivation

I started to hate night, the way it separated me from light,
the way it cut off contact, the sun like a friend I watched
guillotined every evening. I would weep as I saw sunset—

I knew what was coming. The leering moon. The quiet streets.
The occasional car's tires squealing like a pig's cut throat.
The sad blue light of a lonely T.V. buzzing someone into numbness

down the block. Everyone trying to shake off the day and rinse clean,
but night felt dirty to me: water left in a tub, smoke lingering in sheets,
the way unwanted touch remains as though branded onto skin.

Night was three and a half years when the world
closed its eyes as I lost my grip on what rest even was,
when I began to decipher the movements of shadows

like hieroglyphs on the walls that spoke in tongues only I could hear—
my unsleeping daughter crying all night into my eyes,
my inconsolable daughter screaming all night into my mouth.

Self-Portrait with Rain and Memory of Rain

Because tires wheel through puddles in a rush like waves
against a hull and the buds have forced their faces out
of the stems into bright yellow fans and gold clusters
and burgundy tufts like an explosion of delicate sex
in the woods, I can feel myself hovering over everything,
my ghosts alongside me, taking in the wet weather
while the city's patches of green sing their ulterior motives—
cones and pollen, cherry blossoms tongue pink for a moment
and suddenly how they cover the streets, their waxy petals
trodden to pulp. Because I have lived in quieter places than here,
the busses throttling Brighton Avenue with their axels.
Because I have lived closer to trees than this, where I see the woods
from my window, oaks and poplars and pines shivering
in the May rainfall. Always, the separations—glass, window,
wall, fence. Trees as other. Water as means to these ends—
cup of tea. Cup of coffee. But once, I watched raindrops skitter
across car windows, following their movements with my finger.
Because there was the deep splash of puddles during hurricane season,
streets now rivers as big as swimming pools filling the driveways
with scum, the severed arms of the palm fronds reaching out,
the water's skin mottled with more rain. And also there were whole hours
watching rain slow and deep as elephant eyes fill large green leaves,
the rain dripping in a steady rhythm like a waltz. Because I am trying to find it
again, that slow rhythm, the space where I could watch the world between
car rides and groceries and work, the quieting of the trees inside the drip
along leaves cold and wet and full of sky.

Dream of Flying

All that matters is that you start somewhere, choose
something—a cloud, maybe, or a lamppost lit
against the dark like the face of an orchid.
The night is restless, the wind whirls some leaves
that scrape against the empty street like tin spoons.

Start with the lamppost—focus your attention.
You won't have to flap your arms like desperate
wings to lift off—that's beginner's stuff. You soar,
you glide, flight cradles you in its feathered limbs.
For years, you do this, every night. Go outside

and off you'd fly. Above, the moon was a clock face.
Below, the ocean was a vessel of stones.
Your shadow would cast long across the cane fields,
the sky blazing with their burning, or ashen
in the days after. You could hear the mangroves

breathe, storm clouds twisting free of the summer rain
every night on the dot. The way the tropics speak in shivers,
in the underbrush, palm trees alive and plotting, while you,
the conductor, put it all into its restless bed, flying home
in secret, waiting for the next night to begin again.

Fields and Fields

This is still my dream. I speak it into the night
that crawls along the floors, that shares
my bed. There is no loneliness in it, the night

dreams my dream with me. When I speak it
to the walls lilaced by moon they become possible.
How they start: there are fields of lupines

and my daughter is running. There is no rabbit trap
to catch her. There is no threat of neighborhood dogs,
or the cars driving too fast we have become accustomed

to fearing. There is no roar of traffic at all, only wind rushing
over the lupines and my daughter's breathing and her laughter.
A distant bird calls. The lupines bend and sway beneath her

as she runs for the joy of it. There is a house just beyond the field
that belongs to us and it waits for her to dream inside,
for her to touch the walls with her small hands, feel the small smooth bumps

of the cool plaster, to be outside and reach her arms out
and feel with her whole body the field, the sky, the call of the birds
in her ears, to open her mouth and say, "Home."

Galway

Still half drunk, we make our way to the rocky beach tossed in foam, harried by a
storm off to the North. The afternoon stretches out empty, a Thursday on holiday,
scent of whiskey in the waves, of running out of things to say. When the seabirds
make their appearance, hovering over the cliff's lip, time stopped in a plane of sky,
their slight adjustments of feathers and wing so delicate I can't detect them. The small
requires a different kind of attention: raptness, vision described in bird language,
eagle-eyed, sharp as a hawk. I can list the names of seabirds: gulls, terns, cormorants,
albatross, but I'm playing at identification, only knowing names, not qualities, and
my words get muffled in damp like that sea cave we found to have sex in, the floor
littered with shells and bottles, our passion less eager than our desire to avoid injury.
Leaving it behind, always leaving to go somewhere, to that bar, that street, that café,
as though one will provide the piece of ourselves we can't find. I'm so tired. Maybe I
could become the seabirds' imperceptible stilling, holding onto a quiet I've made, the
air pooling around me in a circle. Maybe I could rest in the faint wind, bare as a rock,
making the smallest adjustments— alula, angle of centreline, content to go nowhere.

When I Hold You Close, Your Breath

Is a whisper you push out with your tongue.
You have learned to hush when your mouth
is close to my ear, and your voice is the sea
from the belly of the shell, your voice
is the song I wait to hear each morning, and today
you woke and found me in the bathroom,
wanted to know about my toe—was it ok,
was it hurting me, the toe I might have broken
rushing yesterday to fix your lunch, you,
who you made me rock you as I sat on the toilet
and your whole body was a small petal
cradling my larger petal, like the endless rows
of the crab-apple blossom, or the peony, favorite flowers,
ringed as they are with endless silky tufts
that shatter along the streets, that crown us royal
when we go for our wagon ride to the store,
and the silk of you, the bloom of you, is what
I dream, and the moon of you, the silt of you,
is what I look for when I look anywhere, into
the sky, into the sea, the grit along the road,
the you I made, the you that still wants me near.

What the Dead Wish

Spring grown hot and the neighbors fretting
over their peonies. If given the choice,

I would come back as a tree.
Cherry, spilling over. Almond,

row upon row of velvet drape. Crab-apple,
sinking little boats, like the trees in the fields

outside Cardiff, Wales,
pink fires in the fog.

Those fields of pretending, bending all light
to my lengthening body like wet wood.

How I learned that every tree is a door
to somewhere else,

a leaf-lined road into the dark—bark rimmed with quartz,
wood stark with beetle rot.

Or I could choose the oldest oak to hold my bones.
A small circle of fire. Leaves trampled to dust

on the forest floor, the stars in a dead heat to reach the surface,
where my body used to burn.

But I prefer flowering, the way it mimics
the small hands of children, the frill of filament,

light in the spring dusk. I would press all of my spent life
into some delicate petals as they tumbled from a branch,

honey in a calyx's ripe center, how it all tastes
in the end—blossom and ash.

Field Notes

We have traveled this far: endless rumble of interstate,
four years in Portland with its coastal soot, hemmed in
by rows of houses we cannot afford. Rent each month
liberal politics bumper stickers organic milk scrolling

real estate school pickups, and we have come over a thousand miles
to find what it means to grow—parent, mother, succor, grind,
assume responsibility and make it look effortless. Maybe it is time
to plant ourselves in the rich dark earth and grow the life that's been a seed

all this time—find it Midcoast or further North, near an island
or one of the peninsulas whose fingers drag along the floor
of the Gulf of Maine, find it in Black Sedge, Queen Anne's Lace,
an acre of untamed grasses, framed by woods just right for haunting.

The snap peas will be ready to pick in June, the wood stove done
for the year by then, and my daughter will find a conch shell in
an old shed, blowing into it as if it is the shofar, calling us to come,
to clear, to make this land our own.

Body as Palimpsest

There will be a pause between the waves.
See how they split--they are mica, shale,

they peel away like the shells of shrimp.
They will remind you of yourself stumbling

over chunks of coral at the beach, your acne and dreadlocks,
trailing pencil shavings off the bus in a panic,

will remind you of everything you had wished you were
but weren't –Beirut beautiful, bare as a bomb as it breaks open walls,

ocean wet, small as pistachios— the green ones, the red,
heaped in a Talavera bowl, salt-stiff tongue.

Staining your fingers, wash them off in the sea
that keeps coming at you. Look again, this time,

pencil ready. Your face in the water
is every fish you've seen dart at the bait—

tarpon, *corvina*, lemon shark slow swimming beneath you,
that quiet that roars of nothing, vast and Martian.

In the outer space of the ocean, the shark is the moon,
tugging on the blue of you as if tied to your belly,

and you bob like a geode, looking down. The blue-green waves
so sharp they could cut you with tenderness, the way you crave.

The blue-green waves like the eyes of a stranger. Lapis Lazuli.
Peer into the water, where you are waiting.

You are at the bottom looking up, an oyster,
the sand a bed beneath, the pearl coming, the pearl

that will be born in the tussle of your life, in your body—
you will watch it come, and it will be you.

Acknowledgements

"Afghanistan is Your Fault" was published in *Rattle*

"After a Diagnosis of Postpartum Mood Disorder" was a finalist in the *River Heron Review's* Annual Poetry Contest, 2021

"After Reading Keats 'Ode on Melancholy' in Late February" was published in *Pine Hills Review*

"Animal Dreams" was published in *Pirene's Fountain*

"Aninut" was published in *Small Orange*

"Artists in Quarantine" was published in *Cider Press Review*

"A Walk after Being Let Go" was a finalist in *Sweet Lit's* 2021 Poetry Contest

"Before School There Are Icicles" was the winner of *Sweet Lit's* Annual Poetry Contest, 2021

"Big Ones" was published in *Sandy River Review*

"Brooklyn the Color of a Hospital Gown" was published in *Rust & Moth*

"Chickadee" was published in *Literary Mama*

"Sleep Deprivation" (published as "Post-Partum") was published in *Westchester Review*

"Despite How Much We Say We Hate Winter" was published in *Rejected Lit*

"Everything Grief Can Make You Hold" was published in *Ample Remains*

"First Days" was published as "Powerless" in *Frost Meadow Review*

"Galway" was published in *Entropy*

"Ghost Guns" was published in *Rise Up Review*

"Ghost Story" was published in *The Night Heron Barks*

"How NSSI is a Hammer, a Door, a Knucklebone" was published as "NSSI" in *SWIMM*

"I'm Not Thinking About the End of the World" was published in *River Heron Review*

"Lockdown Day 1,000,000" was published in *Mom Egg Review*

"Mother Mirror" was published in *Oyster River Pages*

"Moths" was published in *Menacing Hedge*

"My Grandmother's Pockets" was published in *Juke Joint*

"Panacea" was published in *South Florida Poetry Journal*

"Poem after Bitter Dreams" was published in *Thimble*

"Pyrocumulonimbus" was published in *Deep Water, Portland Press Herald*

"O Medusa" was published in *Last Leaves*

"Rear-View" was published in *Pirene's Fountain*

"Self-Portrait with Sparrow Song" was published in *Mom Egg Review*

"Self-Portrait with Winslow Homer and Raincoat" (published as "Sailor") was inspired by the painting "Eight Bells" by Winslow Homer and was published in *MWPA ArtWord*, 2021

"Shrine" was published in *Atticus Review*

"Stone Fields with First Snow" was published in *West Trestle Review*

"The Year Our Daughter was Born" was published as "Everything it Took to Make Her" in *Empty House*

"What is Enough" was published in *Inflectionist Review*

"Vaccine Tango with the Red Red Rose" was published in *Global Poemic*

"Loon Stabs Bald Eagle through the Heart the Same Week George Floyd Was Murdered" was published in *Enough! Poems of Protest and Resistance* by Littoral Books

"OCD is Now 'Good Hygiene'" was published in *Wait: A Pandemic Poetry Anthology* by Littoral Books.

For Matthew and Adeline, always.

Multi-Pushcart Nominee, Meghan Sterling has been published or has work forthcoming in *The Los Angeles Review, Rhino Poetry, Colorado Review* and many others. Her first full length collection *These Few Seeds* (Terrapin Books) came out in 2021 and was an Honorable Mention for the 2022 Eric Hoffer Grand Prize in Poetry. Her chapbook, *Self Portrait with Ghosts of the Diaspora* (Harbor Editions) will be out in 2023. Her full-length collection, *Comfort the Mourners* (Everybody Press) will also be coming out in 2023. She is the Program Director at Maine Writers and Publishers Alliance and lives in Maine with her family. Read her work at meghansterling.com.